The HOUGHTON GUIDE to the INTERNET for HISTORY

The HOUGHTON MIFFLIN GUIDE to the INTERNET for HISTORY

Robert Ashley Michael
University of Massachusetts—Dartmouth

HOUGHTON MIFFLIN COMPANY   BOSTON   TORONTO
Geneva, Illinois   Palo Alto   Princeton, New Jersey

Senior Sponsoring Editor: Patricia Coryell
Senior Associate Editor: Jeffrey Greene
Editorial Assistant: Gabrielle Stone
Senior Manufacturing Coordinator: Priscilla Bailey
Marketing Manager: Clint Crockett

About the Author
Robert Ashley Michael is professor of history at the University of Massachusetts, Dartmouth. He is on the staff of H-Net, a humanities electronic network that sponsors and administers many scholarly electronic lists, and is co-moderator of the H-Net lists: H-W-Civ (history of western civilization), HOLOCAUS (Holocaust studies), and H-AntiS (history of antisemitism). Professor Michael is the founder of the UMASSD Internet Users Group and the UMASSD.INTERNAUTS newsgroup. He has also offered electronic courses, seminars, and contributed to many initiatives into the use of computing technology in the humanities.

Acknowledgments
I would like to thank my wife, Susan Ashley Michael, and my nephew, Theodore David Cass, for their help in preparing this manuscript.

Printed in the U.S.A.

ISBN: 0-395-81454-5

123456789-PR–00 99 98 97 96

CONTENTS

INTRODUCTION

The Internet* is an electronic network that connects computers and people all over the globe. Using the Internet allows you—quickly, easily, and either privately or publicly—to communicate electronically with professors and other students, as well as to discover and access a lot of information otherwise inaccessible to you. What I enjoy most about using the Internet is that it leads my mind outside its old parameters into a new world of intellectual and emotional excitement. The Internet is to computers what space travel is to airplanes.

Who runs the Internet? No one. One of the beauties of the net is that no one person or organization controls it. Yet universities, businesses, and institutions of all sorts pay millions of dollars to keep the net running. Thousands of editors working without pay keep things going.

E-MAIL

One of the primary functions of the Internet is e-mail, or electronic mail. E-mail allows you (after you obtain an account on your school's mainframe computer from your school's central computing service) to sit at your own computer or a computer at your school and connect to the 40 million or so people hooked up to the Internet. You can contact any of these people one-on-one, just as in sending a regular letter via U.S. mail (called snail mail); the difference is that you do it electronically, and almost no time elapses between your sending the letter (post) and your addressee receiving it. This can be very important to you. You may want to contact a friend or relative, a professor, a librarian, a fellow student at another school, or one who belongs to a private carrier (like America Online). The problem I was dealing with when I first started using e-mail extensively was my mother's illness. I needed to consult with my brother, a professor in Illinois, on my mother's treatment for cancer. We corresponded via e-mail as many as five or six times a day. On a more mundane level, I contact colleagues, librarians, and administrators about all kinds of issues. My students sometimes contact me to submit papers or to ask questions and obtain advice during my "electronic" office hours.

We have been discussing private correspondence. The other major function of e-mail is to join a public e-mail list. The members of these groups share common interests and communicate among themselves electronically. By joining some of these groups (not all are open to students), you can correspond simultaneously with hundreds of people who are concerned with similar issues. Some groups compose only academics and exclude students; others

---

*See the Glossary at the end of this book for the definitions of new or unfamiliar terms.

combine professors and students; and still others are mostly students. My teenage daughter belongs to X-Files and Michael Jackson lists. I belong to more than a dozen lists, including ones on the Holocaust, classical Greek philosophy, Mark Twain, antisemitism, and the history of western civilization. These lists not only allow you to share your interests but also to gain a lot of information. You can get questions answered. For example, years ago I was listening to the McLaughlin Group on public television, and McLaughlin mentioned a phrase that sounded to me like "hypox legomena." I could not find the phrase in my dictionary, so I contacted the Sophia list because the words sounded Greek. Within a day, I had collected 25 replies to my question. I was informed that the correct phrase was "hapax legomena," which means a one-time-only usage of a term. These e-mail lists are fun as well as enormously interesting and informative. They can help you in the early stages of writing a paper by supplying specific or theoretical information, suggesting bibliographies for material you are seeking in libraries or at Internet sites.

If you use e-mail, you need to know your own e-mail address as well as the e-mail addresses of databases and correspondents. If you use the World Wide Web, you need to know the site address. Each e-mail address consists of three parts: the list's or person's name; the location, which is preceded by an @ sign; and an abbreviation for the kind of network the address originates from. Abbreviations of domains included in e-mail addresses are .edu (educational), .com (commercial), .gov (government), .mil (military), .org (organization), .net (network), and also two-letter country codes (like US for the United States and CH for Switzerland).

Note: You can get overwhelmed, so be careful not to subscribe to too many e-mail lists and newsgroups. Always instruct the list that you want your subscription in digest format so that you will receive only one long comprehensive message from the list instead of dozens of individual posts. To subscribe, send this one-line e-mail message to the listserv address given:

subscribe <name of the list> <Firstname Familyname>

For example, send the following message to listserv@msu.edu:

subscribe h-w-civ Robert Michael

and Robert Michael will be subscribed to the H-Net e-mail list History of Western Civilization. The listserver automatically knows your e-mail address because it is always indicated in the header of your message (post).

You will get a computer-generated response, often followed by a short questionnaire. The editors will sign you up when you return it. The messages will automatically arrive in your e-mailbox.

The Gutenberg Project provides a monthly question-and-answer service for information about the Internet. E-mail gutnberg@vmd.cso.uiuc.edu to join the list.

The World Wide Web site http://www.neosoft.com/internet/paml contains a selection of e-mail lists. Joining these lists can aid your research for term papers by providing the information itself or sending you to the right place to get material on your own. Subjects of use to history students include:

art	history	psychology
Asia	humanities	research
cultural	ideology	societies
economics	literature	weapons
ethics	museums	world
genealogy	political	

The selected e-mail lists noted under the category history are:

EVERYONE'S EINSTEIN, Contact: listserv@idealink.washington.dc.us
HISTORIC COSTUME, Contact: h-costume-request@andrew.cmu.edu
MARHST-L (Maritime History and Maritime Museums List), Contact:
    listserv@qucdn.queensu.ca
NATIVELIT-L (Native American Literature), Contact:
    idoy@crux2.cit.cornell.edu (Michael Wilson)
TITANIC, Contact: jbdavis@nando.net (John Davis)
HLIST (Holocaust Research List) NIZKOR, Contact:
    kmcvay@nizkor.almanac.bc.ca
MEDGAY-L (Medieval Gay men and women), Contact:
    listserv@ksuvm. ksu.edu (Robert Clark)
RENDANCE (Renaissance Dance), Contact: listserver@morgan.ucs.mun.ca

WHO RUNS E-MAIL LISTS?

To give you an idea of who runs e-mail lists, here are a few H-Net lists, along with the names of their moderators or editors and their addresses:

AFRICA: Marcus, Harold, professor of history, Michigan State University,
    22634mgr@msu.edu; and Page, Melvin E., professor of history, East Tennes-
    see State, pagem@etsuarts.east-tenn-st.edu
ANTIS [Antisemitism]: Levy, Rich, associate professor of history, University of
    Illinois, Chicago, rslevy@uic.edu; and Michael, Bob, professor of European
    history, University of Massachusetts, Dartmouth, rmichael@umassd.edu
ASIA: Conlon, Frank, professor of history, University of Washington,
    conlon@u.washington.edu, and Leibo, Steve, associate professor and chair of
    history, Russell Sage College, leibo@albnyvms.bitnet
CIVWAR: Harris, Robert, PhD candidate in history,
    bb05196@bingvmb.cc.binghamton.edu; Knupfer, Peter, associate professor of
    history, Kansas State University, 1@ksu.ksu.edu; and Lowe, Richard, profes-
    sor of history, University of North Texas, fd78@jove.acs.unt.edu
FRANCE: Farr, James, associate professor of history, Purdue University,
    jrfarr@mace.cc.purdue.edu; and Gordon, Bert, professor of history, Mills Col-
    lege, bmgordon@ella.mills.edu

GERMAN: Goda, Norman, assistant professor and chair of history, University of Maine-Presque Isle, goda@polaris.umpi.maine.edu; and Rogers, Dan, assistant professor of history, University of South Alabama, drogers@jaguar1.usouthal.edu

IDEAS: Bledstein, Burt, associate professor of history, University of Illinois, Chicago, BJB@uic.edu; and Bailey, David, associate professor of history, Michigan State University, idea@hs1.hst.msu.edu

TEACH: Kornbluh, Mark, professor of history, Michigan State University, mark@hs1.hst.msu.edu; and Tucker, Sara, professor of history, Washburn University, zztuck@acc.wuacc.edu

WORLD: Manning, Pat, professor of history, Northeastern University, manning@neu.edu; and Segal, Dan, associate professor of history, Pitzer College, dsegal@bernard.pitzer.edu

GOPHER

Gopher is a system that enables the user to find and get (download) items on the Internet. The span of material identifiable by use of the Gopher depends on the administrator who controls the mainframe computer at your school. By means of Gopher menus arranged hierarchically, you can choose item after item until you arrive at the host computer that contains what you are looking for—let's say the card catalog of Brown University's Rockefeller library or the works of William Shakespeare. Some host computers allow you to download material from their directories, that is, transfer files from their computer to yours. For major history Gopher sites, see the section "History Gopher Sites" later in this guide. If your school does not have Gopher installed, you can Telnet to the following public Gopher sites:

consultant.micro.umn.edu
ux1.cso.uiuc.edu
panda.uiowa.edu
gopher.msu.edu

TELNET

Telnet allows you to log into a remote computer and use it as your own for a limited amount of time. You can Telnet to a remote computer at another school, for example, to use the card catalog of that school's library. *Note:* Many schools do not allow outsiders to use their systems unless they have a specific account at that school.

USENET NEWSGROUPS

Not all universities subscribe to the Usenet, a collection of thousands of newsgroups. Newsgroups are like e-mail lists, except that they are usually not moderated, and the membership contains a much higher percentage of students than the more academically inclined e-mail lists. The Usenet is more democratic and, sometimes, more chaotic and anarchic than e-mail lists. Most newsgroups contain a maximum of opinion and a minimum of research material. Some schools limit the number of Usenet groups accessible to students. To join a newsgroup, type **news** at the prompt on your school's mainframe computer, press Enter or Return once, and then type **subscribe <name of the newsgroup>.** Once into news, the command **dir/groups/all** will usually display a list of all the groups kept on your server and available to subscribe to. Since most of the newsgroups are unmoderated, the communications are more casual and frequently outrageous compared to those in e-mail lists. Newsgroup names often run from the general to the specific, for example, soc.cult.jewish.holocaust (society, culture, Jewish, Holocaust). The most common Usenet hierarchies are as follows:

alt. = alternative
bionet. = biology network
bit. = bitnet
biz. = business
comp. = computer
cult. = culture
gnu. = Free Software Foundation
humanities = humanities
info. = information
misc. = miscellaneous
news = Usenet
rec. = recreation
sci. = science
soc. = society
talk = debate

Some Usenet newsgroups that history students can use to obtain information for papers include:

alt.war
alt.war.civil.usa
alt.war.vietnam
humanities.answers
humanities.lit.authors.shakespeare
humanities. misc
misc.news.bosnia
misc.news.east-europe.rferl
misc.news.southasia

news.admin.censorship
news.announce.newgroups
news.groups
news.groups.questions
rec.arts.movies.past-films
rec.food.historic
rec.games.miniatures.historical
rec.travel.europe
soc.culture.afghanistan
soc.culture.african
soc.culture.african.american
soc.culture.albanian
soc.culture.algeria
soc.culture.arabic
soc.culture.argentina
soc.culture.asian
soc.culture.asian.american
soc.culture.assyrian
soc.culture.australian
soc.culture.austria
soc.culture.baltics
soc.culture.bangladesh
soc.culture.belgium
soc.culture.bengali
soc.culture.berber
soc.culture.bolivia
soc.culture.bosna-herzgvna
soc.culture.brazil
soc.culture.british
soc.culture.bulgaria
soc.culture.burma
soc.culture.cambodia
soc.culture.canada
soc.culture.caribbean
soc.culture.celtic
soc.culture.chile
soc.culture.china
soc.culture.colombia
soc.culture.costa-rica
soc.culture.croatia
soc.culture.cuba
soc.culture.czecho-slovak
soc.culture.dominican-rep
soc.culture.ecuador
soc.culture.egyptian
soc.culture.estonia
soc.culture.europe
soc.culture.filipino

soc.culture.french
soc.culture.german
soc.culture.greek
soc.culture.haiti
soc.culture.hongkong
soc.culture.indian
soc.culture.indian.delhi
soc.culture.indian.gujarati
soc.culture.indian.info
soc.culture.indian.kerala
soc.culture.indian.marathi
soc.culture.indian.telugu
soc.culture.indonesia
soc.culture.iranian
soc.culture.iraq
soc.culture.irish
soc.culture.israel
soc.culture.italian
soc.culture.japan
soc.culture.jewish
soc.culture.jewish.holocaust
soc.culture.jordan
soc.culture.korean
soc.culture.kurdish
soc.culture.kuwait
soc.culture.laos
soc.culture.latin-america
soc.culture.lebanon
soc.culture.liberia
soc.culture.maghreb
soc.culture.magyar
soc.culture.malagasy
soc.culture.malaysia
soc.culture.mexican
soc.culture.mexican.american
soc.culture.misc
soc.culture.mongolian
soc.culture.native
soc.culture.nepal
soc.culture.netherlands
soc.culture.new-zealand
soc.culture.nigeria
soc.culture.nordic
soc.culture.pacific-island
soc.culture.pakistan
soc.culture.palestine
soc.culture.peru
soc.culture.polish

soc.culture.portuguese
soc.culture.puerto-rico
soc.culture.punjab
soc.culture.quebec
soc.culture.rep-of-georgia
soc.culture.romanian
soc.culture.russian
soc.culture.scientists
soc.culture.scottish
soc.culture.sierra-leone
soc.culture.singapore
soc.culture.slovenia
soc.culture.somalia
soc.culture.south-africa
soc.culture.south-africa.afrikaans
soc.culture.soviet
soc.culture.spain
soc.culture.sri-lanka
soc.culture.swiss
soc.culture.syria
soc.culture.taiwan
soc.culture.tamil
soc.culture.thai
soc.culture.turkish
soc.culture.ukrainian
soc.culture.uruguay
soc.culture.usa
soc.culture.venezuela
soc.culture.vietnamese
soc.culture.welsh
soc.culture.yugoslavia
soc.culture.zimbabwe
soc.feminism
soc.genealogy.african
soc.genealogy.australia+nz
soc.genealogy.benelux
soc.genealogy.computing
soc.genealogy.french
soc.genealogy.german
soc.genealogy.hispanic
soc.genealogy.jewish
soc.genealogy.marketplace
soc.genealogy.medieval
soc.genealogy.methods
soc.genealogy.misc
soc.genealogy.nordic
soc.genealogy.surnames
soc.genealogy.uk+ireland

soc.history
soc.history.living
soc.history.moderated
soc.history.science
soc.history.war.misc
soc.history.war.us-civil-war
soc.history.war.vietnam
soc.history.war.world-war-ii
soc.history.what-if

WORLD WIDE WEB

The World Wide Web (WWW) is a network of home pages or opening screens with links (click once on a highlighted or underlined letter, word, or phrase) to other screens. These screens, which contain information of all kinds, are in color and often include graphics and sounds. The information available is nearly unlimited in breadth and depth. You can use the Web to access news-groups, Telnet sites, Gopher sites, and FTP sites. *Note:* You must have a fast modem as well as a sophisticated Web browsing or surfing application (Netscape is now the state of the art). See "FTP (File Transfer Protocol)" for a way of obtaining Netscape free. Your school has to have connections to the Web, or you have to hire your own Internet provider and pay a monthly fee. For Web sites of special interest to history students, see "History Web Sites."

It is very easy to find things on the Internet Web. Here is how to start if you already have an Internet address. Click once on the heading OPEN. Then type in an electronic address. A World Wide Web hypertext document is often indicated as follows:

http://<www-site>/<path>/<html-doc>

Here are some popular Web search engines to find material if you have no address:

YAHOO! = http://www.yahoo.com/
LYCOS = http://www.lycos.com/
WEBCRAWLER = http://webcrawler.com

FTP (FILE TRANSFER PROTOCOL)

FTP is an Internet application that allows a user on one computer to access and transfer files to and from another computer over a network. Netscape and other Web browsers automatically use FTP without your having to specify it to download files and applications from another computer. Many sites also allow you to use FTP on your own, without using the Web. You log on as

anonymous and use your e-mail address as your password. *Note:* FTP sometimes requires you to have an account on the computer from which you plan to retrieve a file. You must also know the Internet address of the FTP site, the name of the file you want, the directory in which the file is contained, and a series of FTP commands that require special knowledge. Frankly, because of the complicated commands, I discourage all but the most courageous and persistent of Internauts to use FTP on their own. Compared to the ease of the Web, FTP by itself is archaic. You can download Netscape for free over the Internet on your own by FTPing to ftp.mcom.com/netscape/.

REVIEW: WHAT THE INTERNET ALLOWS STUDENTS TO DO

- Join groups, such as e-mail lists and newsgroups, whose members have similar interests.
- Communicate with thousands of students and faculty all over the world.
- Open up your work to criticism. You can express your opinions on newsgroups and e-mail lists with total freedom and, so long as you are appropriately polite, with impunity. You will receive help, suggestions, and advice from students and faculty all over the world. *Note:* Keep your pieces short and interesting. If you have a long piece, summarize it, or send it in several sections. Don't be put off by the fact that many professors are going to read your material; they love to answer questions—that's their job, after all.
- Gain information about specific facts, databases, and resources through e-mail, Gopher, and the World Wide Web. The Internet allows you to research for information otherwise totally inaccessible to you, over a worldwide collection of libraries and other databases, at almost any time of day or night (daytime working hours are the busiest). *Note:* It is easier to gather bibliographical information than historical data itself. And remember, you need the right equipment. This usually means a computer with a fast modem, at least 14.4 bps (bauds per second) and lots of RAM (4–16MB) and ROM (at least 200MB). Moreover, to download graphics, you need lots of helper applications (see Glossary) besides Mosaic or Netscape or other Web browsers.
- Use e-mail to contact your professors or to submit student papers. *Note:* These uses must be cleared with the professor.
- Discover the enormous variety of human activities not specific to academics that are available through the Internet.

HOW TO GET HOOKED UP

Hardware

You will need a computer—the faster the processor and the more RAM and ROM the better—as well as a modem. The modem allows your digital computer to use the analog phone lines to hook up with another digital computer. Although you will be limited to the speed of your university's modem, 14.4 bps is becoming standard. You can use a terminal at your college that will most likely be all set up with a modem and the correct software to connect to the Internet. Or you can buy this hardware on your own through mail order or at a computer store. Ask around. Perhaps it's best to wait until you arrive at school, when you can take a trip to the bookstore and perhaps buy what you need at a reduced price. Computer magazines and online information also may help you decide what to buy. (Check out the Internet computer index at Gopher proper.com or Netscape to http://ici.proper.com.)

Software

You will need a word processing application—my favorite is Microsoft Word—but lots of good ones are available; perhaps one will come with the computer you buy. You will also need software to connect to the Internet in order to enable your computer to download text and graphics. Internet software may be free on campus, so you should contact central computing.

HOW TO GET STARTED

If you need help, seek out your campus computer guru (see the Glossary), or visit your computer help desk, academic computing service, or the central computer service. On most campuses, you can sign up for an account at central computer service that will allow you to use a university computer or your own computer that is wired to the university mainframe computer, which in turn is probably wired into the Internet. Or else you must purchase a modem and get a software application that will enable you to use the telephone lines to link into your university's mainframe computer. If this is not possible, you can find a local or national service provider that will supply you with software and plenty of instructions so that you can explore the Internet.

H-NET: HUMANITIES ONLINE

A network of 70 scholarly lists for humanists and social scientists, H-Net operates daily newsletters edited by some 140 scholars in North America,

Europe, Africa, and the Pacific. New lists are being added all the time. Subscribers automatically receive messages in their computer mailboxes. These messages can be saved, discarded, downloaded to a PC, copied, printed out, or relayed to someone else. Best of all, the reader can immediately REPLY. There is currently no subscription charge or fee of any kind. *Note:* Some of these lists accept undergraduate subscribers; others do not.

For these lists, send a subscribe message to listserv@uicvm.uic.edu:

H-Antis	Antisemitism
H-Ideas	Intellectual history
H-Italy	Italian history and culture
H-Urban	Urban history
HOLOCAUS	Holocaust studies
IEAHCnet	Colonial; 17th–18th century America

For these lists, send a subscribe message to listserv@msu.edu:

H-Africa	African history
H-Albion	British and Irish history
H-AmRel	American religious history
H-AmStdy	American studies
H-Asia	Asian studies and history
H-Canada	Canadian history and studies
H-CivWar	U.S. Civil War
H-CLC	Comparative literature and computing
H-Demog	Demographic history
H-Diplo	Diplomatic history, international affairs
H-Ethnic	Ethnic, immigration, and emigration studies
H-Film	Scholarly studies and uses of media
H-German	German history
H-Grad	For graduate students only
H-High-S	Teaching high school history and social studies
H-Judaic	Judaica, Jewish history
H-Labor	Labor history
H-LatAm	Latin American history
H-Law	Legal and constitutional history
H-Local	State and local history and museums
H-Mac	Macintosh users
H-MMedia	High-tech teaching; multimedia; CD-ROM
H-NZ-OZ	New Zealand and Australian history
H-PCAACA	Popular Culture Assoc. and American Culture Assoc.
H-Review	H-Net book reviews (reviews only, no discussion)
H-Rhetor	History of rhetoric and communications
H-Rural	Rural and agricultural history
H-Russia	Russian history
H-SAE	European anthropology
H-SHGAPE	U.S. Gilded Age and Progressive Era
H-South	U.S. South

H-Survey	Teaching U.S. survey
H-State	Welfare state; "putting the state back in"
H-Teach	Teaching college history
H-W-Civ	Teaching western civilization
H-West	U.S. West, frontiers
H-Women	Women's history
H-World	World history and world survey texts

For these lists, send a subscribe message to LISTSERV@KSUVM.KSU.EDU:

H-Pol	American politics
H-War	Military history

For these lists, send a subscribe message to
LISTSERV@VM.CC.PURDUE.EDU:

H-France	French history
Habsburg	Austro-Hungarian Empire

For this affiliated list (reviews only, no discussion), write to
Listserv@listserv.acns.nwu.edu:

LPBR-L	Law and politics book review

For this affiliated list, write to h-mexico@servidor.unam.mx:

H-MEXICO	Mexican history and studies

For these affiliated Cliometric Society lists, send a subscribe message to
lists@cs.muohio.edu:

H-Business	Business history (co-sponsored by H-Net)
Databases	Design and management of historical databases
EH.RES	Economic history short research notes and queries
EH.DISC	Economic history extended discussion
EH.NEWS	Economic history news, announcements
EconHist.Macro	Macroeconomic history, business cycles
EconHist.Student	Students and faculty in economic history
EconHist.Teach	Teaching economic history
Global.change	Economic history dimensions of global change
Quanhist.recurrent	Comparative recurrent phenomena

Lists in the planning stage:

H-Af-Am	African-American studies
H-AmInt	American intellectual history
APPALNET	Appalachian studies
H-Japan	Japanese studies
H-MusTex	Lyrical texts; opera
H-RenRef	Renaissance-Reformation

H-SHEAR	Early American Republic
H-Skand	Scandinavian history and culture
H-UCLEA	Labor studies
H-Ukrain	Ukrainian studies

MORE HISTORY LISTS

To subscribe in most cases, send your subscription request to the listserv address as described earlier, not to the list itself. *Note:* Some of these lists accept only graduate students and professors, but that is rapidly changing, and they are now accepting undergraduates as well. Also note that things move very quickly in cyberspace, so some of these lists may be defunct, others may have been created, and a few may have moved to a new e-mail address.

General History

aera-f@asuvm.inre.asu.edu = History and historiography
aibi-l@acadvm1.uottawa.ca = Discussion forum of l'Association internationale bible et informatique
arms-d@xx.lcs.mit.edu = Arms and disarmament
arms-l@buacca.bu.edu = Peace, war, weapons
aseh-l@ttuvm1.ttu.edu = American Society of Environmental Historians
astr-l@uiucvmd.edu = American Soc. for Theatre Research: Theatre History
astro@gitvm1.gatech.edu = Astronomy discussion
bully-l@hearn.nic.surfnet.nl = Bullying and victimization
caah@princeton.edu = Consortium of art and architectural historians
caduceus@beach.gal.utexas.edu = History of the health sciences; history of medicine
census-analysis@mailbase.ac.uk = Census data and related research
census-publications@mailbase.ac.uk = Census reports
chug-l@brownvm.edu = Brown University Computing in the Humanities
classm-l@brownvm.edu = Classical music list
cliology@msu.edu = Theories of history
coins@rocky.er.usgs.gov = Numismatics
comhist@vm.its.rpi.edu = History of human communication
deremi-l@ukanaix.cc.ukans.edu = Military history, especially medieval, but including classical to early modern
dip-d@uwavm.edu = Diplomacy Digest
eca-l@gsuvm1.gsu.edu = European Center-Atlanta of the Institute for East-West Studies
ecchst-l@bgu.edu = A list for the discussion of the history of christianity
econhist@miamiu.acs.muohio.edu = Teaching and research in economic history
ejap@phil.indiana.edu = The Electronic Journal of Analytical Philosophy
ethnohis@hearn.nic.surfnet.nl = General ethnology and history discussion
forced-migration@mailbase.ac.uk = Forced migrations and refugees

gedcom-l@vm1.nodak.edu = Genealogical data
green@indycms.iupui.edu = Green movements
hastro-l@wvnvm.wvnet.edu = History of astronomy in all cultures
hcfnet@ucsbvm.edu = Humanities computing facilities
heritage@massey.ac.nz = Heritage interpretation
histnews@ukanvm.cc.ukans.edu = Historians newsletter
history-all@mailbase.ac.uk = Superlist for mailbase history group lists
history-econ@mailbase.ac.uk = Support for research in worldwide economic
    history
history-ihr@mailbase.ac.uk = Institute of Historical Research
history-methods@mailbase.ac.uk = Computer-based history methods
history-teaching@mailbase.ac.uk = Computers in history teaching
history-news@mailbase.ac.uk = History news
hn-ask-l@ukanvm.cc.ukans.edu = History Network Forum
hn-org-l@ukanvm.cc.ukans.edu = The History Network
htech-l@sivm.si.edu = History of technology
hopos-l@ukcc.uky.edu = History of the philosophy of science
hpsst-l@qucdn.queensu.ca = History and philosophy of science and science
    teaching
humanist@brownvm.edu = Humanities computing list
humgrad@mailbase.ac.uk = Postgraduates working in the humanities
islam-l@ulkyvm.louisville.edu = The history of Islam
islamiat@sakaau03 = Islamic information and issues
l-artech@uqam.edu = Arts and new technologies
l-cha@uqam = Canadian Historical Association
military-history@mailbase.ac.uk = All aspects of military history
milhst-l@ukanvm.cc.ukans.edu = Popular military history
music@finhutc = Music research
muslims@psuvm.psu.edu = Islamic information and news
nahia-l@msu.edu = North American historians of Islamic art
narrative@hg.uleth.ca = Narrative in everyday life
oha-l@ukcc.uky.edu = Oral History Association
ortrad-l@mizzou1.missouri.edu = Comparative oral traditions
peace@indycms.edu = Peace (peace studies)
poli-sci@rutvm1.edu = Political Science Digest
publhist@husc3.harvard.edu = Public history, such as films, museums, serious
    popular history
qual-l@psuvm.psu.edu = Qualitative research
qnteva-l@psuvm.psu.edu = Quantitative research
reach@ucsbuxa.edu = Research and educational applications of computers in
    the humanities
roots-l@vm1.nodak.edu = Genealogy
sharp-l@iubvm.ucs.indiana.edu = History of the printed word
shothc-l@sivm.si.edu = Society for the History of Technology and Computers
sochist@ucbvm.edu = New social history
sochist@vm.usc.edu = New social history (cliometrics)
sos-data@uncvm1.edu = Social science data
stamps@cunyvm.cuny.edu = Philately

textiles@ege.edu.tr = Textiles and clothing studies discussion
un@indycms.iupui.edu = UN (United Nations)
violen-l@bruspvm.edu = Violence
vwar-l@ubvm.cc.buffalo.edu = Vietnam war discussion
war-research-sources@mailserv.ac.uk = Research sources for study of war, peace, and defense
wmst-l@umdd.umd.edu = Discussion of women's studies issues
world-l@ubvm.cc.buffalo.edu = Non-eurocentric world history
wsn@csf.colorado.edu = World systems
wwii-l@ubvm.cc.buffalo.edu = World War II discussion

Asia

actmus-l@ubvm.cc.buffalo.edu = Serious Asian contemporary music
asia-l@gsuvm1.gsu.edu = Regents' Asian Center
australia-nz-history-l@coombs.anu.edu.au = History of Australia and New Zealand and contacts with Asia
buddha-l@ulkyvm.louisville.edu = Buddhist academic discussion
cenasia@mcgill1.ca = Central Asia politics
cps-l@hearn.nic.surfnet.nl = Center for Pacific Studies
e-asia-area-group@coombs.anu.edu.au = Research School of Pacific Studies
pacarc-l@wsuvm1.csc.swu.edu = Pacific Rim archaeology

Korea and Japan

emjnet@magnus.acs.ohio-state.edu = Early modern Japan. To subscribe, write pbrown@magnus.acs.ohio-state.edu
japan@pucc.princeton.edu = Japanese Business and Economics Network
jpinfo-l@jpnsutoo = Information about Japan
jpop@ferkel.ucsb.edu = Japanese popular culture and music
jtem-l@uga.cc.uga.edu = Japanese through electronic media
jtit-l@psuvm.psu.edu = Japanese language teaching and technology
nihongo@mitvma.mit.edu = Discussion of Japanese language
origami@cs.utexas.edu = Discussion of origami

China

acmr-l@uhccvm.uhcc.hawaii.edu = Chinese music research
ccnet-l@uga.cc.uga.edu = Technologies relating to use of Chinese on computers and word processing
china@pucc.princeton.edu = Chinese studies discussion
china-l@ucf1vm.edu = Florida-China Linkage Institute discussion
china-link@ifcss.org = Chinese Academic Link
china-nd@kentvm.kent.edu = China News Digest, United States
china-nn@utarlvm1.uta.edu = China News Digest, Global
china-nt@uga.cc.uga.edu = Independent Federation of Chinese Students and Scholars

chinalaw@listserv.ncsu.edu = Chinese legal and administrative history
chinanet@tamvm1.tamu.edu = News on networking in China
chinese@kenyan.edu = Teachers, researchers, and students of the Chinese language
chpoem-l@ubvm.cc.buffalo.edu = Chinese classical and modern poems
cmc-bulletin@ifcss.org = Center for Modern China Bulletin
cmc-forum@ifcss.org = Center for Modern China Forum
csg@listserv.ncsu.edu = Chinese studies group
emedch-l@vm.usc.edu = Early Medieval China list
taoism-l@coombs.anu.edu.au = Information and scholarly discussion of Tao and Taoism
tibet-l@iubvm.ucs.indiana.edu = Tibet and Tibetan people discussion
ttwsim-l@im.mgt.ncu.edu.tw = Taiwan Society for Information Management, Taiwan
zenbuddhism-l@coombs.anu.edu.au = Nature and history of Zen Buddhism

Southeast Asia

avsl-l@coombs.anu.edu.au = Scholarly and factual information on science and technology relevant to Vietnam
berita-l@vmd.cso.uiuc.edu = News of Malaysia, Singapore, Islam
ids@suvm.syr.edu = Indonesian development studies
misg-l@psuvm.psu.edu = Malaysian Islamic affairs
permika@vm1.mcgill.ca = Indonesian development studies
seanet-l@nusvm.nus.sg = Southeast Asian studies
seasia-l@msu.edu = Southeast Asia discussion
vn-dict@saigon.com = Vietnamese dictionary

India and Pakistan

buddhist@jpntuvm0.edu = Indian and Buddhist studies
currents@pccvm.edu = South Asian News and Culture Magazine
hindu-d@arizvm1.ccit.arizona.edu = Hindu Digest
india@cunyvm.cuny.edu = India List
india-d@vm.temple.edu = India News and Discussion
india-d@ukcc.uky.edu = India News and Discussion
india-d@utarlvm1.uta.edu = India News and Discussion
india-l@ukcc.uky.edu = India News Network
india-l@vm.temple.edu = India News Network
india-l@utarlvm1.uta.edu = India News Network
indology@liverpool.ac.uk = Classical India discussion
nepal@mp.cs.niu.edu = Nepal Digest
pakistan@asuvm.inre.asu.edu = Pakistan News Service
pakistan@psuvm.psu.edu = Pakistan News Service
pns-l@psuvm.psu.edu = Pakistan News Service discussion
sagar-journal@bongo.cc.utexas.edu = Electronic journal of South Asian studies
tamil-l@um.urz.uni-heidelberg.de = Tamil Studies
telugu@vm1.nodak.edu = World Telugu People network

Near East

ane@oi.uchicago.edu = Pre-Islamic ancient Near East
heblang@israel.nysernet.org = Hebrew grammar and etymology
ir-net@irearn.ir = Computer networking in Iran
itisalat@guvm.ccf.georgetown.edu = Arabic language and technology
meh20-l@taunivm.tau.ac.il = Discussion of water research in Middle East
newsflash@israel.nysernet.org = Mideast news from Israel
pafnet@acfcluster.nyu.edu = Palestinian academic
persia-l@emuvm1.cc.emory.edu = Jewish literature and history
ptt-l@ege.edu.tr = Turkish issues

Africa

africa-l@brownvm.brown.edu = Pan-Africa Forum
africa-l@gsuvm1.gsu.edu = Pan-Africa Forum
africa-l@vtvm1.cc.vt.edu = Pan-African Forum
africa-n@vm.utcc.utoronto.ca = Africa News and Information Service
africana-l@listserv.cc.wm.edu = Information technology and Africa
algnews@gwuvm.gwu.edu = Algerian news
egypt-net@cs.sunysb.edu = Egyptian heritage, history, and culture
miast-l@vmd.cso.uiuc.edu = Maghrebian Scientific Institute
naijeduc-l@usq.edu.au = Higher education in Nigeria
swahili-l@macc.wisc.edu = Readers and writers of Kiswahili
tssact-l@utkvm1.utk.edu = Tunisian Scientific Society
tssnews@psuvm.psu.edu = Tunisian Information Office, Washington
tunisnet@psuvm.psu.edu = Tunisia Network

Ancient Europe

aegeanet@acpub.duke.edu = Aegean bronze-age and classical archaeology
ancien-l@ulkyvm.louisville.edu = History of the ancient Mediterranean
bmcr-l@cc.brynmawr.edu = The Bryn Mawr Classical Review
classics@uwavm.u.washington.edu = Greek and Latin Classics
elenchus@acadvm1.uottawa.ca = Christian thought and literature in late
    antiquity
ellhnes@cs.wisc.edu = Hellenic Society
ioudaios@vm.utcc.utoronto.ca = First-century Judaism and early Christianity
latin-l@psuvm.psu.edu = Classical, medieval, and neo-Latin language, literature
sophia@liverpool.ac.uk = Ancient philosophy
thuc-l@vm.temple.edu = Thucydides

Middle Ages

ansax-l@wvnvm.wvnet.edu = Anglo-Saxon and Old English studies, 450–1100
arthurnet@morgan.ucs.mun.ca = Arthurian subjects
assisi-l@auvm.american.edu = Franciscan list
bmmr-l@cc.brynmawr.edu = The Bryn Mawr Medieval Review

byzans-l@mizzou1.missouri.edu = Byzantine studies

camelot@castle.ed.ac.uk = Arthurian discussion

chaucer@unlinfo.unl.edu = The works of Geoffrey Chaucer and medieval English literature and culture, 1100–1500

celtic-l@irearn.ucd.ie = Celtic culture

dante's divine comedy = DANTE's Telnet address: library.dartmouth.edu. At the login, type CONNECT DANTE

earlym-l@aearn.edvz.uni-linz.ac.at = Early music discussion

erasmus = Renaissance and Reformation studies. To subscribe, write bowen@vm.epas.utoronto.ca

ficino@vm.utcc.utoronto.ca = Center for Reformation Studies, 1350–1700

gerlingl@vmd.cso.uiuc.edu = Older (to 1500) Germanic languages

hislaw-l@ulkyvm.louisville.edu = History of law (feudal, common, canon)

history-vasco@mailbase.ac.uk = 15th–16th century Portuguese discoveries

interscripta@morgan.ucs.mun.ca = Medieval studies

mdvlphil@lsuvm.sncc.lsu.edu = Medieval philosophy and sociopolitical thought

med-and-ren-music@mailbase.ac.uk = Medieval and Renaissance music

medevlit@siucvmb.siu.edu = Medieval English literature

medfem-l@uwavm.u.washington.edu = Medievalist feminists

medgay-l@ksuvm.ksu.edu = Gay–lesbian issues in medieval studies

mediev-l@ukanvm.cc.ukans.edu = Medieval history

medievale@uqam.ca = Medieval history (in French)

medliteracy@uclink.berkeley.edu = Medieval literacy

medsci-l@brownvm.brown.edu = Medieval and Renaissance science

medtext-l@vmd.cso.uiuc.edu = Medieval literature and textual studies

perform@iubvm.ucs.indiana.edu = Medieval performing arts

reed-l@vm.utcc.utoronto.ca = Feudal English drama, music, ceremony

renais-l@ulkyvm.louisville.edu = History of the Renaissance

rendance@morgan.ucs.mun.ca = Renaissance dance

shaksper@vm.utcc.utoronto.ca = Shakespeare Electronic Conference

text@vinga.hum.gu.se = Old Swedish texts

tml-l@iubvm.ucs.indiana.edu = Latin music theory

East and Central Europe

balt-l@ubvm.cc.buffalo.edu = Baltic republics

baltj-l@mizzou1.missouri.edu = Journalism in the Baltic countries

cas@listserv.ncsu.edu = Area studies of former Soviet Union

cerro@awinu11.edvz.univie.ac.at = Central European Regional Research Organization

donosy@ndcvx.cc.nd.edu = Polish affairs

e-europe@pucc.princeton.edu = CEE/CIS business and economic systems

east-west-research@mailbase.ac.uk = Social, economic, and political transformation in Central and Eastern Europe and the former Soviet Union

eochr-l@qucdn.queensu.ca = Eastern Orthodox Christianity

h-net@huearn.sztaki.hu = Hungarian Academic and Research Network

hungary@gwuvm.gwu.edu = Hungarian discussion
mideur-l@ubvm.cc.buffalo.edu = Middle Europe
orthodox@iubvm.ucs.indiana.edu = Orthodox Christianity
pigulki@acsu.buffalo.edu = Polish news and humor magazine
poland-l@ubvm.cc.buffalo.edu = Polish culture and events
rferl-l@ubvm.cc.buffalo.edu = Latest developments in the former Soviet Union
    and Eastern Europe
rusag-l@umdd.umd.edu = Russian agriculture
rushist@earn.cvut.cz = Russian history forum, 1462–1917
rushist@vm.usc.edu = Russian history
rushist@umrvmb.umr.edu = Russian history
russia-studies@mailbase.ac.uk = Former Soviet Union and Eastern Europe
seelangs@cunyvm.cuny.edu = Slavic and East European languages and litera-
    ture
slovak-l@ubvm.cc.buffalo.edu = Slovak issues
sovhist@earn.cvut.cz = Soviet history, 1917–1991
sovhist@umrvmb.umr.edu = Soviet history forum
tps-l@indycms.iupui.edu = Soviet politics
ukraine@indycms.iupui.edu = Ukraine

Western Europe (after 17th century)

9nov89-l@tuvbm.cs.tu-berlin.de = The Berlin Wall
aatg@indycms.iupui.edu = Teachers of German
albion-l@ucsbvm.edu = British history
austen-l@mcgill1.ca = Jane Austen and her contemporaries
balzac-l@cc.umontreal.ca = French culture
blake@albion.com = William Blake
c18-l@psuvm.psu.edu = 18th-century interdisciplinary studies
caci-l@vm.ucs.ualberta.ca = Canada and Italy
campinas@pccvm.icc.pcc.edu = Portuguese language
cins-l@vm.ucs.ualberta.ca = Canadian-Scandinavianists
classm-l@brownvm.brown.edu = Classical music list
dickens-l@ucsbvm.edu = Charles Dickens forum
ec@vm.cc.metu.edu.tr = European Community
emhist-l@rutvm1.rutgers.edu = Early modern history
englit-victorian@mailbase.ac.uk = Victorian literature
espana-l@uacsc2.albany.edu = Spain and its peoples
espora-l@ukanvm.cc.ukans.edu = History of Iberian peninsula
francehs@uwavm.u.washington.edu = French history scholars
frogprof@bitnic.educom.edu = American Association of Teachers of French
fwake-l@irlearn.ie = Finnegan's Wake
gemcs-l@vaxc.hofstra.edu = Western and eastern early modern culture
germnews@vm.gmd.de = German news
h-italy@uivcm.uic.edu = History of Italy
habsburg@vm.cc.purdue.edu = Austrian history since 1500
hegel@villvm.edu = Friedrich Hegel

hellas@psuvm.psu.edu = Hellenic discussion list
hellas@uga.cc.uga.edu = Hellenic discussion list
hesse-l@ucsbvm.edu = Herman Hesse
hume-l@listserv.cc.wm.edu = David Hume
iberia@mailbase.ac.uk = Spanish and Portuguese studies
ireland@rutvm1.rutgers.edu = Discussion of the news and articles from and
    about Ireland
irl-news@rutvm1.rutgers.edu = News and articles from and about Ireland
irl-pol@irlearn.ucd.ie = Current Irish politics
irtrad-l@irlearn.ucd.ie = Irish traditional music
italia-l@irlearn.ucd.ie = Discussion for Italianists
j-joyce-request@cc.utah.edu = James Joyce
langit@icineca.it = Italian culture and language
law-europe@mailbase.ac.uk = European law
litera-l@tecmtyvm.mty.itesm.mx = Literature in English and Spanish
ln-fr@fromp11.cnusc.fr = Langage naturel de France
low-country-l@mac.dartmouth.edu = History and culture of Netherlands and
    Belgium, 4th–20th century
mail-ita@vm.cnuce.cnr.it = Electronic mail in Italy
mgsa-l@cmsa.berkeley.edu = Modern Greek studies
mendele@yalevm.cis.yale.edu = Yiddish literature and language
milton-l@urvax.edu = Discussion of the life and literature of John Milton
modbrits@kentvm.kent.edu = Modern British and Irish literature from 1895
nassr-l@wvnvm.wvnet.edu = Romanticism
tolkien@jhuvm.edu = J. R. R. Tolkien readers
victoria@iubvm.ucs.indiana.edu = Nineteenth-century British culture and soci-
    ety
welsh-l@irlearn.ucd.ie = Welsh language bulletin board
wig-l@cmsa.berkeley.edu = Feminist study of German literature, language, and
    culture

Americas in General

amercath@ukcc.uky.edu = History of American catholicism
american-studies@mailbase.ac.uk = U.K. academics working in American stud-
    ies
canchidd@vm.utcc.utoronto.ca = NAFTA and economic issues in Canada, Mex-
    ico, and the United States
labor-l@vm.utcc.utoronto.ca = Labor in western hemisphere
mclr-l@msu.edu = Midwest Consortium for Latino Research

Caribbean, Latin America, and South America

boriken@enlace.pr = Cultura y Sociedad de Puerto Rico
bras-net@pccvm.icc.pcc.edu = Brazil
canalc@vm.utcc.utoronto.ca = Canadian Association for Latin-American and
    Caribbean Studies

carecon@vm.utcc.utoronto.ca = Caribbean economy
cdsbc-l@ufrj.br = Conselho da Sociedade Brasileira
centam-l@ubvm.cc.buffalo.edu = Central America discussion
ch-ladb@unmvm.unm.edu = Latin-America database
chickle@unmvm.unm.edu = Chicano literature discussion
chile-l@utarlvm1.uta.edu = Chile discussion
chilehoy@usachvm1.usach.cl = Diario del acontecer en Chile
colext@andescol.uniandes.co = Los Colombianos en el Exterior
comedia@arizvm1.ccit.arizona.edu = Hispanic classic theater
cread@vm.utcc.utoronto.ca = Latin-American and Caribbean Electronic Distance Education
cuba-l@unmvma.unm.edu = Cuba today
ecocarib@conicit.ve = Economias del Caribe
econom-l@ibm.ufsc.br = Economia Brasileira
foro-l@arizvm1.ccit.arizona.edu = Transborder library forum
haiti-l@conicit.ve = Recherche en Haiti
iberam@vinga.hum.gu.se = Ibero-American countries
inter-ch@uschvm1.usach.cl = Internet—Chile
pgkpking@cyber.widener.edu = Journal of Afro-Latin American Studies and Literatures
ladig.-l@unmvma.unm.edu = Latin-America database interest group
laspau-l@harvarda.harvard.edu = Latin-American scholarship program of American universities
latam-info@mailbase.ac.uk = Latin-American studies
latino-l@amherst.edu = Latino students' network
mclr-l@msu.edu = MidWest Consortium for Latino research
mexico@itesmvf1.rzs.itesm.mx = Noticias de Mexico
mexico-l@tecmtyvm.mty.itesm.mx = Mexican people, places, culture
mpb-l@brufpb.br = Lista para musica popular Brasileira
nahuat-l@acc.fau.edu = Aztec/Nahuatl studies
noticol@andescol.uniandes.co = Noticias de Colombia
poesia@unalcol.unal.edu.co = Poesia Latinoamericana
politica@ufrj.br = Discussoes sobre a Politica Brasileira
redalc@frmop11.cnusc.fr = Reseau Amerique Latine et Caraibes
rehred@frmop11.cnusc.fr = Reseau telematique Haitien pour la Recherche
rmclas@unmvma.unm.edu = Rocky Mountain Council for Latin-American Studies
salsa@conicit.ve = Integracion cientifica y cultural del area de Caribe
sm-ladb@unmvm.unm.edu = Latin-America database
up-ladb@unmvm.unm.edu = Latin-America database

North America

aacuny-l@cunyvm.cuny.edu = Asian-American culture
ads-l@uga.cc.uga.edu = American Dialect Society
afam-l@mizzou1.missouri.edu = African-American research
afas-l@kentvm.kent.edu = African-American Studies and Librarianship

afrex@afrex.uucp.edu = African-American forum for Afrocentrism
afroam-l@harvarda.harvard.edu = African-American life and culture
amlit-l@mizzou1.missouri.edu = American literature
amwest-h@vm.usc.edu = History of the American West, 1809–1890
asa-l@tamvm1.tamu.edu = African-American Student Association
assnet-l@uhupvm1.uh.edu = African-American Student Network
baptist@ukcc.uky.edu = Baptist experience, thought, activities
blacklib@guvm.ccf.georgetown.edu = Conference of Black Librarians
canada-l@vm1.mcglll.ca = Canadian issues
datpers@vm.utcc.utoronto.ca = Dalit and tribal peoples
earam-l@kentvm.kent.edu = Society of Early Americanists
franklin@ncsuvm.edu = Benjamin Franklin Scholars
histech@ulkyvm.cc.ukans.edu = History of evangelical Christianity
indians@suvm.syr.edu = Cultural activities of the Indian Assoc.
iroquois@vm.utcc.utoronto.ca = Iroquois language
jazz-l@vm.temple.edu = Jazz list
miles@hearn.nic.surfnet.nl = Miles Davis discussion
nat-1492@tamvm1.tamu.edu = Columbus Quincentenary
pnwcsc@uwavm.u.washington.edu = Pacific Northwest Canadian
prezhist@kasey.umck.edu = U.S. presidential history
shaker@ukcc.uky.edu = The United Society of Believers
soco-l@ubvm.cc.buffalo.edu = Southern rock music
t-amlit@bitnic.educom.edu = Teachers of American literatures
twain-l@vm.utcc.utoronto.ca = Mark Twain
westam-l@yalevm.cis.yale.edu = Western Americana

INTERNET COUNTRY CODES

Afghanistan = AF
Albania = AL
Algeria = DZ
American Samoa = AS
Andorra = AD
Angola = AO
Anguilla = AL
Antarctica = AQ
Antigua and Barbuda = AG
Argentina = AR
Armenia = AM
Aruba = AW
Australia = AU
Austria = AT
Azerbaijan = AZ
Bahamas = BS
Bahrain = BH

Bangladesh = BD
Barbados = BB
Belarus = BY
Belgium = BE
Belize = BZ
Benin = BJ
Bermuda = BM
Bhutan = BT
Bolivia = BO
Bosnia and Herzegovina = BA
Botswana = BW
Brazil = BR
British Indian Ocean Territory = IO
Brunei = BN
Bulgaria = BG
Burundi = BI

Cambodia = KH
Cameroon = CM
Canada = CA
Cape Verde = CV
Cayman Islands = KY
Central African Republic = CF
Chad = TD
Chile = CL
China = CN
Colombia = CO
Comoros = KM
Congo = CG
Cook Islands = CK
Costa Rica = CR
Cote d'Ivoire = CL
Croatia = HR
Cuba = CU

Cyprus = CY
Czech Republic = CZ
Denmark = DK
Djibouti = DJ
Dominica = DM
Dominican Republic = DO
East Timor = TP
Ecuador = EC
Egypt = EG
El Salvador = SV
Equatorial Guinea = GG
Estonia = EE
Ethiopia = ET
Falkland Islands = FK
Faroe Islands = FO
Fiji = FJ
Finland = FL
France = FR
French Guiana = GF
French Polynesia = PF
French Southern Territories = TF
Gabon = GA
Gambia = GM
Georgia = GE
Germany = DE
Ghana = GH
Gibraltar = GL
Greece = GR
Greenland = GL
Grenada = GD
Guadeloupe = GP
Guam = GU
Guatemala = GT
Guinea = GN
Guyana = GY
Haiti = HT
Honduras = HN
Hong Kong = HK
Hungary = HU
Iceland = IS
India = IN
Indonesia = ID
Iran = IR
Iraq = IQ
Ireland = IE
Israel = IL

Italy = IT
Jamaica = JM
Japan = JP
Jordan = JO
Kazakhstan = KZ
Kenya = KE
Korea, Democratic People's Republic of = KP
Korea, Republic of = KR
Kuwait = KW
Kyrgyzstan = KG
Lao People's Democratic Republic = LA
Latvia = LV
Lebanon = LB
Lesotho = LS
Liberia = LR
Libya = LY
Liechtenstein = LI
Lithuania = LT
Luxembourg = LU
Macau = MO
Madagascar = MG
Malawi = MW
Malaysia = MY
Maldives = MV
Mali = ML
Malta = MT
Marshall Islands = MH
Martinique = MQ
Mauritania = MR
Mauritius = MU
Mexico = MX
Micronesia (Federated States of) = FM
Moldova, Republic of = MD
Monaco = MC
Mongolia = MN
Montserrat = MS
Morocco = MA
Mozambique = MZ
Namibia = NA
Nepal = NP
Netherlands = NL
Netherlands Antilles = AN
New Caledonia = NC

New Zealand = NZ
Nicaragua = NI
Niger = NE
Nigeria = NG
Norfolk Island = NF
Northern Mariana Islands = MP
Norway = NO
Oman = OM
Pakistan = PK
Palau = PW
Panama = PA
Papua New Guinea = PG
Paraguay = PY
Peru = PE
Philippines = PH
Pitcairn = PN
Poland = PL
Portugal = PT
Puerto Rico = PR
Qatar = QA
Reunion = RE
Romania = RO
Russian Federation = RU
Rwanda = RW
St. Helena = SH
Saint Kitts and Nevis = KN
Saint Lucia = LC
St. Pierre and Miquelon = PM
Saint Vincent and the Grenadines = VC
Samoa = WS
San Marino = SM
Saudi Arabia = SA
Senegal = SN
Seychelles = SC
Sierra Leone = SL
Singapore = SG
Slovakia = SK
Slovenia = SL
Solomon Islands = SB
Somalia = SO
South Africa = ZA
Spain = ES

Sri Lanka = LK
Sudan = SD
Suriname = SR
Swaziland = SZ
Sweden = SE
Switzerland = CH
Syrian Arab Republic =
    SY
Taiwan, China = TW
Tanzania, United Re-
    public of = TZ
Thailand = TH
Togo = TG
Tonga = TO

Trinidad and Tobago =
    TT
Tunisia = TN
Turkey = TR
Turks and Caicos Is-
    lands = TC
Uganda = UG
Ukraine = UA
United Arab Emirates =
    AE
United Kingdom = GB
United States = US
Uruguay = UY
Uzbekistan = UZ

Vatican City State (Holy
    See) = VA
Venezuela = VE
Vietnam = VN
Virgin Islands (U.K.) =
    VG
Virgin Islands (U.S.) =
    VI
Western Sahara = EH
Yemen = YE
Yugoslavia = YU
Zaire = ZR
Zambia = ZM
Zimbabwe = ZW

HISTORY WEB SITES

American Memory at the Library of Congress:
    http://rs6.loc.gov/amhome.html

Association for History and Computing, Groningen, The Netherlands:
    http://grid.let.rug.nl/ahc/

Cardiff's Movie Database:
    http://web.cm.cf.ac.uk/movies/moviequery.html

Chronicle of Higher Education:
    http://chronicle.merit.edu

Civil War Archives:
    http://www.access.digex.net/~bdboyle/cw.html
    http://jefferson .village.virginia.edu/vshadow/vshadow2.html

Demography Statistics:
    http://opr.princeton.edu (link to data archive through European Fertility
    Project)

European History:
    http://ihr.sas.ac.uk:8080/ihr/ihr0101.html

Global Network Navigator:
    http://gnn.com/gnn/gnn.html

Higher Ed Web Pages List
    (more than 1,000 college and university web page locations):
    http://web.mit.edu:8001/people/cdemello/univ.html

History Index:
   http://history.cc.ukans.edu/history/index.html

Ihr-Info (Institute for Historical Research), London:
   ihr.sas.ac.uk:8080/ihr/ihr0101.html

International Affairs Resources:
   http://web.pit.edu/~ian/ianres.html

Military History:
   http://lcweb.loc.gov
   http://kuhttp.cc.ukans.edu/history/milhst

Mississippi State Page:
   http://web.msstate.edu/archives/history/index.html

NOW Home Page:
   http://now.org/now/home.html
   Chronicle of Higher Education: http://chronicle.merit.edu

Ohio State History Home Page:
   http://web.acs.ohio-state.edu/humanities/history/histdep.html

Paleolithic Cave Painting Graphics:
   http://web.culture.fr/culture/gvpda-en.html

Presidential Libraries:
   http://www.yahoo.com/reference/libraries/presidential-libraries

Spy Satellite Photos:
   http://edcweb.cr.usgs.gov/dclass/dclass.html

State History Home Page:
   http://web.acs.ohio-state.edu/humanities/history/histdep.html

T-Amlit Home Page (Teaching American Literature):
   http://web.georgetown.edu/tamlit/tamlit-home.html

United Nations Development Databases:
   http://web.undp.org

University of Kansas Sources:
   http://kuhttp.cc.ukans.edu/history/web_history_main.html or
   http://kuhttp.cc.ukans.edu/history/hnsource_main.html

World History Standards Debate:
   http://neal.ctstateu.edu/history/world_history/archives/stndrds.html

World War 2 Photos:
   http://www.webcom/~jbd/ww2_pictures.html

HISTORY GOPHER SITES

American Historical Documents:
  gopher.micro.umn.edu
  info.umd.edu
  wiretap.spies.com
  quartz.rutgers.edu
  gopher://joeboy.micro.umn.edu:70/11ebooks/by%20title/histdocs
  gopher://dewey.lib.ncsu.edu:70/11/library/stacks/historical-documents-US

Canadian History:
  gopher://porpoise.oise.on.ca:70/11/eloise/refdesk/documents

CIA World Factbook:
  sunny.stat-usa.gov/11/stat-usa/ntdb/wofact

H-Net Gopher:
  gopher.uic.edu

Historical Documents:
  euler.math.usma.edu
  Telnet: ukanaix.cc.ukans.edu.

Medieval:
  gopher://gopher.lib.virginia.edu:70/11/alpha/bmmr
  wiretap.spies.com

University of Michigan Resources:
  una.hh.lib.umich.edu
  For subject-oriented Internet resources, go to:
  una.hh.lib.umich.edu/11/inetdirs

OBI, The Online Book Initiative:
  email address = obi@world.std.com or
  Gopher to world.std.com

Oxford Text Archive:
  Both literary and nonliterary texts. This list can be obtained by sending the
  message:
  SEND OXFORD SHORTLIST
  to:
  archive@vax.oxford.ac.uk

President (presidential libraries connections):
  sunsite.unc.edu
  Web: http://sunsite.unc.edu/lia/president

Russian and Soviet History:
  gopher://una.hh.lib.umich.edu:70/11/newstuff/exp/slavic

A clearinghouse for subject-oriented internet resource guides at the University of Michigan: This is a searchable index. It may be reached as follows:
Gopher to gopher.lib.umich.edu, choose "What's New" and then "Clearinghouse, etc."
Telnet to una.hh.lib.umich.edu 70
Web to http://www.lib.umich.edu/cchome.html
Several of these guides are of interest to students of history, for example, Black/African studies, West European history and culture

Rice University has collected Internet resources by subject matter. Categories historians may be interested in include:
history
government, political science, and law
military science
music
news and journalism
religion and philosophy
sociology and psychology
Gopher to riceinfo.rice.edu
Web to http://riceinfo.rice.edu/
Jughead and Veronica may be used to search out information here. Check out: "Information by Subject Area."

INTERNET GLOSSARY

You can learn a lot about history and computers, as well as the Internet, by reading this glossary straight through. These abbreviations are used in e-mail, Usenet, and World Wide Web communications, that is, in Internet messages.

AFK   Away from keyboard.

alias   A name, usually short and easy to remember, that is translated into another name, usually long and difficult to remember.

alt.   A hierarchy of newsgroups in the Usenet devoted to alternative interests.

anonymous FTP   Anonymous FTP allows you to retrieve documents, files, programs, and other archived material from anywhere on the Internet. To the host computer's question, Username, answer: anonymous. To the host computer's question, Password, answer: <your e-mail address>.

Appletalk   A networking protocol developed by Apple Computer for communication between Apple Computer products and other computers.

Archie   A Research Check of Hierarchically Indexed Emissions. An application that gives you the location of information on the Internet. You must Telnet to an archie server, for example, Telnet archie.ans.net. Logon with archie. Use archie to find where a file is located, and then use FTP to obtain the file. Archie searches for software by matching your searchword with names and locations.

E-mail to: archie@<servername>.
Some archie servers:
archie.au   (Australia)
archie.edvz.uni.lin.c.at (Austria)
archie.univie.ac.at (Austria)
archie.cs.mcgill.ca (Canada)
archie.uqam.ca (Canada)
info.funet.fi (Finland)
archie.univ.rennes1.fr (France)
archie.ac.il (Israel)
archie.th-darmstadt.de (Germany)
archie.unipi.it (Italy)
archie.wide.ad.jp (Japan)
archie.hana.nm.kr (Korea)
archie.internic.edu (New Jersey)
archie.sura.net (Maryland)
archie.rutgers.edu (New Jersey)
archie.ans.net (NY and all over the world)
archie.nz (New Zealand)
archie.uninett.no (Norway)
dorm.rutgers.edu (Rutgers University)
archie.rediris.es (Spain)
archie.luth.se (Sweden)
archie.switch.ch (Switzerland)
archie.ncu.edu.tw (Taiwan)
archie.doc.ic.ac.uk (United Kingdom)
archie.hensa.ac.uk (United Kingdom)
archie1.unl.edu (University of Nevada)

archive site A computer that provides entry to a collection of files accessible through the Internet.

ASCII American Standard Code for Information Interchange. Standard text with little or no formatting. Also called plain vanilla.

baud The number of times your modem changes its signal per second.

BinHex A Macintosh program that converts binary files sent over the Internet to ASCII files.

Birds of a Feather (BOF) A Birds Of a Feather (flocking together) is an informal discussion group with a narrow focus.

Bitnet Because It's Time Network. An academic computer network that provides interactive electronic mail and file transfer services. It uses the Internet but is now rather outmoded.

bomb A crash of your computer system.

boot To start up one's computer, like pulling yourself up by your own bootstraps.

BRB Be right back.

browser An application that allows you to visit Web sites. Also called a surfer.

BTW By the way.

bye One of the quit commands.

CARL The Colorado Alliance of Research Libraries. An index of thousands of journals.

case sensitive Internet applications that distinguish between uppercase and lowercase letters in commands.

CD-ROM Compact Disk-Read Only Memory. Compact disks that store large amounts of data.

CERN Conseil Européen pour la Recherche Nucléaire. Swiss creators of the World Wide Web.

chat Simultaneous communication over the Internet.

client A computer system or process that requests a service of another computer system or process. A workstation requesting the contents of a file from a server is a client of the server.

clueless newbie Hostile term for a newcomer to the Internet.

compress To squash a file so that it takes up less memory.

cracker An individual who attempts to access computer systems without authorization. These individuals are often malicious, as opposed to hackers, who are benign computer geeks.

cyberspace An often used word coined by William Gibson in his book *Neuromancer* to describe the imaginary reality of a world of computers.

dialup A temporary, as opposed to dedicated, connection between machines established over a standard phone line.

discussion group An online group of people dedicated to one topic via e-mail, newsgroup, or IRC.

distribution list An alias assigned to a list of e-mail addresses.

Domain Name System DNS Its principal use is in Internet addresses. Some important domains are .com (commercial), .edu (educational), .net (network), .gov (U.S. government), .mil (U.S. military), and .org (nonprofit organization).

dot In Internet addresses, the period (as in .com) is always referred to as a dot.

download To transfer a file from a larger computer to a desktop computer.

dump To transfer data from one computer to another for storage or to print.

electronic mail e-mail A system whereby a computer user can exchange messages with other computer users (or groups of users) via a communications network. To e-mail is to post messages on the Internet.

emoticons These signs, viewed sideways, are used to express the writer's emotions: a smiley :-), a winkey ;-), a boohoo :-(

FAQ Frequently asked questions. Several e-mail and Usenet groups allow access to files containing FAQ and their answers.

File Transfer Protocol FTP A protocol that allows a user on one computer to access and transfer files to and from another computer over a network. To do so, you must have an account on the computer from which you plan to retrieve a file. You must also know the Internet address of the FTP site, the name of the file you want, and the directory in which the file is contained. Many sites allow you to logon as anonymous and to use your e-mail address as your password.

finger An unhappily named program that displays information about a particular user, or all users, logged on a computer system. It typically shows full name, last login time, idle time, terminal line, and terminal location. It may also display material indicated by the user so fingered.

flame A strong, sometimes obscene, opinion or criticism of something in an electronic mail message.

freenet Community-based bulletin board system with e-mail, information services, interactive communications, and conferencing.

FWIW For what it's worth.

FYI For your information.

geek Someone who knows a lot about computers or the Internet. Not necessarily a derogatory term.

GIF Graphic Interchange Format. An application that enables you to download graphic images onto your desktop computer stored originally on another computer that you reach through an Internet application.

gigabyte Gig About one billion bytes. Many computers today are equipped with a hard drive that contains a gigabyte or more of storage.

Gopher An internet software application that makes available hierarchical collections of information across the Internet. Gopher gets its name from the mascot of the University of Minnesota, where the service was developed. The gopher is also a burrowing animal, which, more or less, describes the function of the service. It is also a pun on the word *gofer*, someone whose job is to get things.

guru Someone who knows, and knows he or she knows, a lot more than you do about computers and the Internet.

hacker A person who delights in having an intimate understanding of the internal workings of computers and computer networks. The term refers to benign behavior, in contrast to the malignant cracker.

header The portion of an e-mail post preceding the actual message. It contains source and destination addresses, date and time, and so on.

helper applications   Programs like Sparkle and JPEG that enable Netscape to download graphics.

home page   The starting page at a Web site.

host   A computer that allows users to communicate with other computers on the Internet. Individual users communicate by using application programs, such as electronic mail, Telnet, and FTP.

HTML   Hypertext markup language used on Web pages that provides links to other Web sites.

IBM   Most think this abbreviation stands for International Business Machines, but Macintosh users see it as, I believe in Macintosh.

IMHO   In my humble opinion.

IMNSHO   In my not so humble opinion.

IMO   In my opinion.

Internaut   Someone who surfs or browses the Internet.

Internet   A collection of interconnected computers and computer networks that can be reached via an electronic address.

Internet Relay Chat   IRC A worldwide Internet "party line" that allows you to "talk" with others in real time.

IOW   In other words.

jargon file   A dictionary of hacker slang.

JPEG   An application that transmits compressed images and then decompresses them.

Jughead   Jonesy's Universal Gopher Hierarchy Excavation And Display. Searches the menus on a Gopher all at once.

K   KB, Kbyte A kilobyte, or 1,024 bytes. A measurement of memory storage.

Kermit   A once popular, but now relatively slow, file transfer developed at Columbia University.

listserver   A computer application that manages the mail sent to subscribers of a list; an automated electronic mail room. Note the difference between a listserver and the list itself, which consists of the people reading the information. To subscribe to an e-mail list, send a message to the listserver; to interact with other members of the list, send a message to the list name.

Local Area Network   LAN A very fast data network intended to serve an area of only a few square kilometers or less.

LOCIS   Library of Congress Information Service. Available via e-mail at locis.loc.gov or marvel.loc.gov and via Web to http://www.loc.goor http://lcweb.loc.gov.

lurking   A member of an e-mail list lurks when he or she does not participate in the dialogue of the e-mail list or newsgroup. A person who is lurking just reads the discussion. Beginners should lurk until they get the gist of what's going on.

luser A hacker's term for a clueless newbie.

mailing list A list of e-mail addresses of people with a common interest. A mailing list may be moderated in that messages, or posts, sent to the list are actually sent to a moderator who determines whether or not to forward the messages to everyone else. Requests to subscribe to, or leave, a mailing list should *always* be sent to the list's "request" address, usually a listserver.

Mb Megabit, or 1,048,576 bits of information transmitted per second, as over a modem. A bit is a binary digit, the smallest unit of computer data.

MB Meg Megabyte, or 1,048,576 bytes of information stored on a hard drive or RAM memory.

modem An electronic device that connects your computer over the telephone lines to all other computers.

moderator A person, or small group of people, who manage moderated mailing lists and newsgroups. Moderators are responsible for determining which e-mail submissions are passed on to the list.

Mosaic An application from NCSA (National Center for Supercomputer Applications) at the University of Illinois that enables you to surf the WWW.

MUD Multiuser domain. An interactive Internet game environment. Also called fugue, MOO, Muck, MUSE.

netiquette A pun on "etiquette" referring to proper behavior on the Internet.

Netscape The state-of-the-art Web surfer.

network A computer network is a data communications system that connects computer systems at various sites.

newbie A newcomer to the Internet.

newsgroup A Usenet discussion group.

no carrier Message displayed on computer screen when the modem connection between your computer and other computers is disconnected. It usually leads to gnashing of the teeth.

offline No longer connected to the Internet.

OIC Oh, I see.

oldbie A veteran user of the Internet.

online Connected to the Internet.

Online Computer Library Catalog UCLC A nonprofit membership organization offering computer-based services to libraries, educational organizations, and their users.

OTOH On the other hand.

PLOKTA Press lots of keys to abort. What a newbie does to quit while still in insert mode.

post An e-mail message.

postmaster   The person responsible for taking care of electronic mail problems, answering queries about users, and other related work at a site.

Post Office Protocol (POP)   A protocol that allows users to read mail from a server.

Project Gutenberg   An organization that publishes, over the Internet, classic works of literature that are out of copyright. Its e-mail address is gutnberg@vmd.cso.uiuc.edu (the missing "e" is not a mistake).

protocol   An agreed-on format for two different kinds of computers or software to communicate with each other over the Internet.

queue   A backup of messages awaiting processing.

RAM   Random access memory. Most machines today come equipped with 4–16 MB of RAM. Memory that any application or process can read or write to.

remote login   Operating on a remote computer as though locally attached.

ROM   Read-only memory. Fixed memory on a hard drive.

RSN   Real soon now (an event that may never happen).

RTFAQ   Read the FAQ.

server   A computer hooked into the Internet that automatically provides information, such as file servers and name servers.

SIG   Special interest group of computer users on the Internet.

signature   The three- or four-line message at the bottom of a piece of e-mail or a Usenet article that uniquely identifies the sender. Large signatures (more than five lines) are frowned upon.

SITD   Still in the dark.

snail mail   Ordinary U.S. mail. A term that is critical of the speed of the U.S. Postal Service.

sneakernet   Copying material onto a floppy disk and then walking over to another computer to copy it on the hard drive.

spam   Automatically posting a message to nearly an unlimited number of Internet recipients. From a Monty Python skit highlighting and repeating the word *spam*.

subscribe   To join an e-mail group or start reading a newsgroup.

surf   To investigate the Internet, especially the Web. To browse.

sysop   A computer bulletin board operator.

TANSTAAFL   There ain't no such thing as a free lunch.

TCP/IP Protocol Suite   Transmission Control Protocol over Internet Protocol. This application enables your computer to connect to the Internet.

Telnet   A computer program that permits real-time interaction with distant host computers. It is used to search online library catalogs or similar information servers. It is also possible to use it to access Web, Archie, or Gopher sites.

TIA Thanks in advance.

TIC Tongue in cheek.

Trojan Horse A computer program that carries within itself a means to allow the creator of the program access to the system using it.

TTFN Ta-ta for now.

uncompress To expand a compressed file.

URL Uniform Resource Locator. An address for FTP site, Gopher server, Telnet, or especially, the Web. It consists of a protocol, host name, port, directory, and file name.

Usenet A collection of thousands of topically named newsgroups, the computers that run them, and the people who read and submit news. Also called Newsnet.

username The name you logon with. Also the first part of an Internet address (it ends at the @).

Vax Virtual Address Extension. A DEC (Digital Equipment Corp.) computer.

Veronica Very Easy Rodent-Oriented Netwide Index to Computerized Archives. Searches all the Gopher menus (that is, Gopherspace) for titles of files. You can then instruct Veronica to take you to the actual material that you want, and it will—usually.

virtual Something that exists only in computer software.

virus A destructive program hidden inside a benign one that replicates itself on computer systems.

Wide Area Information Servers WAIS Retrieves information from networked databases. WAIS searches for contents of documents, rather than just titles. To use WAIS, Telnet to one of these servers:
info.funet.fi (log in as INFO)
quake.think.com (log in as SWAIS)
sunsite.unc.edu (log in as SWAIS)
swais.cwis.uci.edu (log in as SWAIS)
wais.com (log in as WAIS)
wais.nis.garr.it (log in as SWAIS)

World Wide Web WWW Also known as the Web. A linked collection of hypertext documents (Web pages) collected on Web servers created by researchers at CERN in Switzerland. Users may create, edit, or browse hypertext documents with a single click of the mouse. The clients and servers are freely available. Web browsers can connect you to Gopher, FTP, and Telnet sites and newsgroups, and can send e-mail. The Web connects you to databases and searches them. It can retrieve textual information, as well as graphics, moving pictures, and sound.

worm A computer program that replicates itself. Worms, as opposed to viruses, are meant to spawn in network environments.

WYSIWYG What you see is what you get.